LADBABY

BIOGRAPHY

THE JOURNEY OF MARK & ROXANNE HOYLE, OUR FAVORITE SOCIAL MEDIA COUPLE

Caro Jenny Sullivan

Content

Part I: The Foundation Years

Chapter 1: Working Class Heroes

Nottingham Roots

Born on April 12, 1987, Mark Ian Hoyle's early life in Nottingham laid the groundwork for his future success. The working-class values of this East Midlands city ran through his veins. His childhood centered around Greythorn Primary School, where he would later return as a successful author to inspire a new generation.

Football provided an escape during these formative years - Mark held a season ticket at Nottingham Forest Football Club, sitting in the same spot from age six. This passion for the club would later influence his son's middle name, showing how deeply these early experiences shaped his future.

Early Challenges

School life presented significant hurdles for young Mark. He faced severe bullying, an experience that left lasting scars on his confidence. The effects lingered well into adulthood - years later, when starting his content creation career, Mark initially refused to appear on camera.

"I was like, 'I hate the sound of my own voice, I hate how my teeth look, it's never something I'll do,'" he later revealed to The Guardian. These insecurities, born from childhood trauma, took years to overcome.

Learning Different

Both Mark and Roxanne faced additional academic challenges through their dyslexia. This learning difference made their educational achievements even more remarkable. Their shared experience with dyslexia later influenced their approach to children's literature, creating books that spoke to all types of learners. It also fueled their determination to succeed in creative industries where written communication played a central role.

Breaking New Ground

The significance of their university attendance cannot be understated. As first-generation students from working-class backgrounds, both Mark and Roxanne carried the weight of family expectations. "I struggled at university," Mark admitted frankly. The transition from their working-class backgrounds to academic life presented cultural and social challenges that many of their peers never faced.

Creative Callings

The advertising industry seemed a natural fit for their creative talents, but it too presented class-based obstacles. Roxanne excelled as an art director, while Mark built his career in graphic design. Their different roles gave them complementary skills - her eye for visual storytelling and his technical abilities would later combine perfectly for content creation. Yet even in these successful careers, they encountered prejudice. "I struggled in advertising," Mark noted, highlighting the ongoing class barriers in creative industries.

Rising Through Ranks

Roxanne's talent shone particularly bright in advertising. She rose to become the higher earner in their relationship, proving her abilities in a competitive field. This achievement carried extra weight given her working-class background and dyslexia - two factors that might have held back someone with less determination.

Building Experience

The advertising world taught them valuable lessons about creativity, communication, and connecting with audiences. They learned how to craft messages that resonated with people, skills that would prove invaluable in their future career. Their experience handling client briefs and meeting deadlines prepared them for the demands of content creation, though they didn't know it at the time.

Class Consciousness

Their backgrounds shaped their approach to success. Coming from families where university education wasn't the norm, they understood the value of hard work and authenticity. These working-class values - staying true to yourself, remembering where you came from, helping others up the ladder - would later define their public persona and guide their charitable work.

Early Influences

The creative industries exposed them to both opportunities and limitations. They witnessed firsthand how class could affect career progression, even in supposedly meritocratic fields. This experience fueled their later determination to remain authentic despite success, to maintain their working-class identity even as their circumstances changed.

The foundation years shaped not just their professional capabilities but their entire worldview. Mark's experiences with bullying and self-doubt would later transform into the confidence to entertain millions. Roxanne's creative talents would find new expression in their shared digital ventures.

Their working-class backgrounds and shared experience as first-generation university students gave them a perspective on success that set them apart from many of their peers in the entertainment industry. These early challenges and triumphs created the resilience they would need for their unexpected rise to fame.

Chapter 2: A Las Vegas Love Story

Creative Connection

The British advertising industry in the early 2010s brought together two talents who would reshape social media entertainment. Mark Hoyle, a graphic designer with a keen eye for visual storytelling, and Roxanne Messenger, a talented art director, found themselves working in the same creative circles.

Their first meeting lives on in a photograph they've kept - a snapshot that captured the beginning of a partnership that would influence British popular culture.

Professional Chemistry

Their shared background in advertising created an immediate connection. Both understood the pressures of creative work, the challenges of client deadlines, and the satisfaction of seeing ideas come to life.

Their complementary skills - her art direction expertise and his design abilities - formed a solid foundation for collaboration. Roxanne's role as an art director had already established her as a rising talent, while Mark's graphic design work showed his ability to connect with audiences.

Making It Official

In May 2015, Mark and Roxanne made a decision that reflected their spontaneous approach to life - they eloped to Las Vegas. The choice to marry away from traditional British wedding expectations set the tone for their future decision-making. By choosing their own path rather than following convention, they demonstrated the independence that would later characterize their content creation style.

Financial Reality

Returning to England as newlyweds, the Hoyles faced practical challenges head-on. Their combined income from advertising provided stability, with Roxanne's position as art director bringing in the higher salary. This period of dual-income security wouldn't last long, but it gave them time to establish their married life and plan for the future.

Early Decisions

The advertising world had taught them valuable lessons about creativity and communication, but it also showed them the limitations of traditional career paths. Their working-class backgrounds gave them a practical approach to financial planning - they knew the value of every pound earned and the importance of preparing for unexpected changes.

Family Planning

Within months of their Vegas wedding, the couple received news that would alter their life trajectory - they were expecting their first child. This announcement brought joy but also forced difficult decisions about their professional futures. The high cost of childcare in Britain would soon push them to reconsider their career paths entirely.

Hard Choices

Despite Roxanne's higher income, the couple calculated that her entire salary would barely cover childcare costs. This realization led to one of their first major decisions as parents-to-be: Roxanne would leave her successful advertising career to care for their coming child. The choice meant adapting to life on Mark's single salary, a situation that would test their resourcefulness.

Building Home

Their early married life centered on creating a stable home environment while managing increasingly tight finances. The transition from two professional incomes to one brought unexpected challenges. They had to adapt quickly, learning to stretch every pound and find creative solutions to everyday problems - skills that would later form the basis of their content creation.

Finding Balance

The pressure of supporting a family on a single income weighed heavily on Mark, though he tried to hide his concerns. "I was terrified," he later admitted. "I was the only one bringing the money, and it wasn't enough." Yet even during these challenging times, they maintained their sense of humor, using laughter to lighten difficult situations.

Their experience in advertising had taught them to think outside conventional boundaries. This mindset served them well as they faced the realities of living on a reduced income. They began developing money-saving strategies and practical solutions that would later become the foundation of their social media content.

As they prepared for parenthood, neither Mark nor Roxanne could have predicted how their circumstances would push them toward social media stardom. Their focus remained on the immediate challenges: preparing for their baby's arrival, managing their budget, and supporting each other through the changes ahead. The skills they'd gained in advertising - creativity, adaptability, and the ability to connect with audiences - would soon find new expression in ways they hadn't imagined.

The Vegas wedding that seemed spontaneous had actually laid the groundwork for their future success. Their willingness to take risks, trust their instincts, and support each other through challenges would prove invaluable in the years ahead.

Chapter 3: From Crisis to Creativity

The Hard Math

2016 brought the Hoyles face-to-face with Britain's childcare crisis. The numbers told a stark story - childcare costs rivaled mortgage payments, and Roxanne's entire art director salary would barely cover the expense. The choice became clear but painful: maintaining two careers would cost them money. This realization forced their hands, leading to Roxanne's departure from advertising despite her position as the higher earner.

The transition to a single income hit hard. After paying bills and essentials, the Hoyles had just £20 per week for food. Roxanne approached grocery shopping with military precision, armed with a calculator in Aldi. "I'd go round Aldi with a calculator," she later recalled to The Guardian. One moment stood out - when she went 70 pence over budget at checkout. A stranger's kindness saved the day with a pound coin, a memory that stayed with her through their later success.

Silent Struggles

The pressure of sole financial responsibility weighed heavily on Mark. "I was terrified," he later confessed. "I was the only one bringing the money, and it wasn't enough." These fears remained unspoken at the time. "I don't think I truly shared with you how it made me feel," he would later tell Roxanne, "because I didn't want it to look like I wasn't coping."

Finding Light

Despite the financial strain, the Hoyles turned to humor as their coping mechanism. "You'd try to make a joke," Mark explained, reflecting on their approach to hardship. "It's what my family did when I was little, and it's always got us through everything." This ability to find humor in difficult situations would later become their trademark.

A Forest Grows

In 2016, their son Phoenix Forest arrived. The middle name paid tribute to Nottingham Forest Football Club, Mark's beloved team since childhood. The name choice reflected their deep connection to their roots, even as they faced new challenges as parents. Mark's dedication to work meant missing Phoenix's first steps - an absence that would later influence their career decisions.

Creative Spark

During Roxanne's pregnancy, Mark noticed something missing in the parenting content landscape. "I was like, I want to read the bloke that owns a chippy and has three kids, the everyday bloke that's talking about being a dad," he explained. This gap in representation sparked an idea. As the first among his friends to become a father, Mark created a Facebook page called "LadBaby" - reflecting his transition from "lad" to father.

Starting Small

The early days of LadBaby showed little hint of future success. Mark's initial goal was modest -

he hoped to catch a baby brand's attention and secure some free nappies. The page gained about 1,000 followers through photo posts with captions, but growth seemed slow. Mark nearly abandoned the project before making a crucial decision to try video content.

Breaking Barriers

Creating videos meant confronting deep-seated insecurities from Mark's experiences with childhood bullying. "I was like, 'I hate the sound of my own voice, I hate how my teeth look, it's never something I'll do,'" he recalled. Yet necessity proved stronger than fear. Using a free editing app - the same one they would continue using years later - Mark created his first video.

Finding Their Voice

The combination of practical parenting tips and humor struck a chord with viewers. Their content spoke directly to families facing similar financial pressures, offering both practical solutions and emotional support through laughter. The authenticity of their struggle-to-success story resonated with audiences tired of polished parenting influencers.

Building Momentum

While success didn't come overnight, each piece of content built their following. Their experience in advertising helped them understand their audience and craft engaging content. The skills they'd developed in their corporate careers - creativity, communication, and connecting with audiences - found new expression in social media.

The transformation from struggling young family to social media stars began in these difficult moments. Their financial hardships, rather than defeating them, sparked creativity and determination. The LadBaby brand emerged from genuine need - the need to save money, the need to connect with other parents, the need to find humor in hard times. These authentic beginnings would shape their entire approach to content creation and set the stage for their unprecedented success.

Part II: The Rise

Chapter 4: Going Viral

The Video That Changed Everything

June 2017 marked a turning point in the Hoyles' story. Using a basic free editing app, Mark created a video showcasing his solution to an everyday parenting challenge - a £4 toolbox transformed into a child's lunchbox. This simple idea, born from financial necessity, resonated with parents across Britain. The video demonstrated their core appeal: practical solutions delivered with humor and authenticity.

The creation of this first viral video represented more than just clever content - it marked Mark's triumph over deep-seated insecurities. "I think that's what LadBaby did for me personally: it helped with my confidence," he later shared with The Guardian. The success of the toolbox video proved that relatability mattered more than polished perfection.

Early Innovation

The Hoyles' creative problem-solving didn't stop at lunchboxes. Their content expanded to include a baby walker crafted from pipes, a makeshift paddling pool fashioned from a skip, and a DIY baby gate created from half a door. Each solution showcased their ability to find affordable answers to common parenting challenges.

Valentine's Viral Moment

February 2018 brought another breakthrough when the couple orchestrated mutual Valentine's Day surprises. They each had the other's car wrapped with love heart stickers and photographs of their faces. The resulting videos captured their natural chemistry and playful relationship, earning massive engagement across social media platforms.

The Power of Authenticity

Their content stood out in the crowded parenting influencer space through its raw honesty. Mark continued using the same free editing app that created their first viral hit, proving expensive equipment wasn't necessary for engaging content. This commitment to accessibility reflected their broader message about affordable parenting.

Finding Their Voice

"Yes, mate!" emerged organically from Mark's natural enthusiasm, becoming their signature catchphrase. The expression captured their approachable, down-to-earth style, making viewers feel like they were watching friends rather than content creators. This authenticity set them apart from more polished influencers.

Growth Strategy

By October 2018, their following had grown so substantially that expansion became necessary. They launched LadBaby & Sons, a second YouTube channel featuring their children more prominently. The new channel focused on toy testing and family-friendly challenges, showing their understanding of content diversification while maintaining their core values.

Building Community

Their social media presence expanded rapidly across platforms. The main YouTube channel attracted over 1 million subscribers, while their Facebook page reached 4.9 million followers. Their Instagram following grew to 1.3 million. These weren't just numbers - they represented a community of parents who found comfort and humor in the Hoyles' content.

Professional Transition

Despite their growing social media success, Mark maintained his graphic design job for two years after their first viral hit. This cautious approach demonstrated their practical nature - only when their monthly social media earnings surpassed Mark's annual salary did they commit fully to content creation.

Content Evolution

Their approach to content remained consistent even as their platform grew. Three weekly live sessions with paying subscribers created direct connections with their audience. Their decision to manage their own social media accounts, rather than hiring teams, maintained the authentic voice that attracted followers.

Platform Expansion

As their following grew, they adapted their content for different platforms while maintaining their core message. Facebook showcased their parenting hacks, YouTube carried their longer-form content, and Instagram shared glimpses of their daily life. Each platform received tailored content while maintaining their signature style.

Their success proved that authenticity could compete with production value, that humor could coexist with practical advice, and that social media could build genuine communities.

Chapter 5: Building the Brand

Digital Empire

By late 2018, LadBaby had transformed from a simple parenting blog into a multi-platform phenomenon. Their following grew to 13 million across social media platforms, with three weekly live sessions attracting paid subscribers. The numbers represented more than statistics - they showed how relatability and authenticity could build genuine connections in the digital age.

Family Growth

2018 brought another milestone with the arrival of their second son, Kobe Notts. The middle name, like his brother Phoenix Forest's, paid homage to their Nottingham roots. The addition of Kobe added new dimensions to their content, showing the realities of parenting multiple children while maintaining their signature humor and practical approach.

Content Philosophy

The Hoyles established clear boundaries around their children's involvement in social media. "We're always reviewing it," Mark explained in media interviews. "We let them judge whether or not they want to be involved - we don't force them." This approach explained why their older son appeared more frequently in videos than their younger one, who showed less interest in being filmed.

Professional Recognition

October 2019 marked a significant milestone when they signed deals with WME and MVE Management. These partnerships opened new opportunities while allowing the Hoyles to maintain their authentic voice. The same month, they released their first book, "Parenting for £1: ...And Other Baby Budget Hacks," bringing their money-saving tips to print.

Family First

The attic room in their Nottingham house became their recording studio, allowing them to balance content creation with family life. This setup meant they could maintain consistent output while staying present for their children's milestones - a stark contrast to their corporate days when Mark missed Phoenix's first steps.

Award-Winning Parents

Their approach to parenting content earned widespread recognition. In June 2018, Mark won Clas Ohlson's "Celebrity Dad of the Year" award, beating Prince William in a public vote. Nine months later, Roxanne claimed the "Celebrity Mum of the Year" title, cementing their status as relatable parenting figures.

Brand Values

Despite growing success, the Hoyles maintained their budget-conscious mindset. Roxanne continued shopping at Poundland and Home Bargains, while they drove standard cars rather than luxury vehicles. This commitment to modest living reinforced their message about practical parenting and responsible spending.

Content Management

Unlike many influencers, the Hoyles chose to manage their own social media accounts. This hands-on approach meant seeing all comments - positive and negative - but preserved their direct connection with followers. Their decision to maintain control over their content distinguished them from creators who outsourced engagement.

Monetization Strategy

Their business model focused on accessibility and authenticity. Rather than chasing high-end sponsorships, they sought partnerships that aligned with their values. This approach resonated with their audience, who appreciated their continued focus on affordable solutions even as their own circumstances improved.

Educational Impact

Their content evolved to include more educational elements alongside entertainment. They demonstrated how everyday situations could become teaching moments, whether through money-saving tricks or practical parenting tips. This blend of education and entertainment would later influence their children's book series.

Brand Expansion

November 2019 saw the publication of their first book, extending their influence beyond social media. The book's success proved their appeal could translate across media platforms, setting the stage for future ventures. Their ability to maintain their voice and values while expanding their brand showed remarkable consistency.

The foundation they built during this period - clear values, strong boundaries, authentic content - would support their next phase of growth. Their commitment to reliability and practical solutions had created more than a following; it had built a community.

Chapter 6: Breaking Records

The First Note

In 2018, the Hoyles took an unexpected turn into music with a simple goal: help food banks. At the time, 14 million people in Britain lived below the poverty line. The connection was personal - Roxanne's mother volunteered at a food bank, and they remembered their own struggles living on £20 weekly food budgets. Their solution combined British humor with charitable giving: a novelty Christmas song about sausage rolls.

December 14, 2018, saw the release of "We Built This City" - their sausage roll-themed parody of Starship's 1985 hit. The song faced tough competition from established artists, including Ava Max's "Sweet but Psycho" and Ariana Grande's "Thank U, Next." Against these odds, LadBaby secured the Christmas number one spot, becoming the first British YouTubers to top the charts.

Rolling Forward

Buoyed by their initial success, 2019 brought "I Love Sausage Rolls," transforming "I Love Rock 'n' Roll" into another pastry-themed hit. Nick Southwood joined the project, co-writing lyrics with the Hoyles while handling production, mixing, and instrumental performances. The single's cover art paid homage to The Beatles' Abbey Road, foreshadowing their future connection to the Fab Four's Christmas record.

Three Times Lucky

2020's "Don't Stop Me Eatin'" - their take on Journey's "Don't Stop Believin'" - featured sleeve artwork referencing Queen's Bohemian Rhapsody. A duet version featuring Ronan Keating and Roxanne added star power to their charitable effort. The single sold 158,000 copies in its first week, with 94% coming from paid-for sales rather than streams, becoming the fastest-selling single since 2017's Grenfell Tower charity record.

Star Power

2021 marked their most ambitious project yet - collaborating with Ed Sheeran and Elton John on "Sausage Rolls for Everyone." The recording sessions created surreal moments. "Sitting in a studio seeing Elton John singing lyrics you've written in your living room - lyrics about sausage rolls - is just wild," Mark recalled. The experience showed how far they'd come from their first parody attempt.

Breaking Records

Their final Christmas single, 2022's "Food Aid," completed their historic run. Five consecutive Christmas number ones - surpassing The Beatles' record of four (achieved in 1963, 1964, 1965, and 1967). This achievement stood as a testament to both their popularity and their charitable impact.

Charitable Impact

By December 2022, their Christmas singles had raised £305,000 for The Trussell Trust. Combined with their brand partnerships, the total reached £1,305,000. The charity itself confirmed these figures, highlighting the real-world impact of their musical endeavors.

Global Tradition

Their Christmas singles created an international phenomenon. Families worldwide, from Australia to America, gathered to listen to the chart countdown. The Hoyles had created more than hits - they'd established a holiday tradition that connected people across continents.

The Final Note

In 2023, the Hoyles announced they wouldn't release another Christmas single. Though Roxanne hinted at a possible return for their 10-year anniversary in 2028, suggesting "a sausage roll megamix," their record-breaking run had concluded. Their impact on British music history was secured.

Industry Recognition

Their achievements earned multiple entries in British music history. They became one of the few acts to top the charts with their first three singles. Even their dramatic chart drops set records - including one single falling from number one to number 78, establishing the biggest drop within the UK Top 75.

Legacy

What started as a charitable idea turned into a historic achievement. The Hoyles proved that authenticity, humor, and good intentions could compete with mainstream music industry power. Their success opened new doors, but it also brought unexpected challenges. The spotlight grew brighter, and with it came increased scrutiny and pressure that would test their resilience.

The LadBaby Christmas singles phenomenon changed both music industry expectations and charitable giving. They showed how social media influence could translate into mainstream success, and how novelty songs could serve serious purposes. Their five-year run of Christmas number ones set a record that might never be broken, while raising over £1 million for food banks - proving entertainment and social responsibility could work hand in hand.

Part III: Impact & Legacy

Chapter 7: The Trussell Trust Partnership

The Reality of Hunger

The numbers tell a stark story of modern Britain. By 2023, The Trussell Trust provided 3.1 million food parcels in a single year - a 94% increase over five years. Behind these statistics stood real families, working parents, and children facing hunger. The Hoyles understood this reality intimately, remembering their own days of stretching £20 for a week's groceries.

Roxanne's mother worked as a food bank volunteer, giving the couple a direct window into Britain's growing hunger crisis. Through her experiences, they learned that food poverty touched all segments of society. This personal connection would shape their future charitable work in ways they couldn't have anticipated when starting their social media career.

Breaking Stereotypes

Through their volunteer work at Nottingham food banks, the Hoyles witnessed how hunger affected people from all walks of life. "There's this perception - or there certainly used to be - that it was really just the homeless that used food banks," Mark explained in interviews. "And what we see is it's not: it can be nurses, it can be people working two jobs, whole family units coming in after school just to get their food parcel."

The First Campaign

The 2018 release of "We Built This City" marked their first major fundraising effort. The decision to donate proceeds to The Trussell Trust came naturally - they knew the organization's work firsthand. At the time, 14 million people in Britain lived below the poverty line. The Hoyles saw an opportunity to use their platform for meaningful change.

Growing Impact

Their Christmas singles campaign grew year after year. By December 2022, The Trussell Trust confirmed the Hoyles had raised £305,000 through their Christmas singles alone. When combined with their brand partnerships, the total reached £1,305,000. Each pound represented direct support for families facing food insecurity.

Brand Partnerships

October 2020 saw the Hoyles partner with Walkers to create limited-edition sausage roll-flavored crisps. Five pence from each packet went to The Trussell Trust, extending their fundraising beyond music. This collaboration showed how they leveraged their growing platform to create additional revenue streams for the charity.

Publishing with Purpose

Their commitment to fighting hunger extended into their publishing ventures. By 2024, their "Greg the Sausage Roll" series included charitable components, with portions of sales supporting The Trussell Trust. Their February 2024 book release committed donations up to £10,000 through WHSmith sales.

Real Faces of Need

St Margaret's the Queen Church in Brixton became a powerful symbol of their impact. Home to the Norwood and Brixton Food Bank, it served as the filming location for their acoustic version of "Sausage Rolls for Everyone." They recorded alongside stroke survivor Donna Kennedy and her 12-year-old son Ronan, putting real faces to the stories of those helped by food banks.

Facing Criticism

Their charitable work attracted scrutiny. Despite The Trussell Trust's confirmation of their donations, the Hoyles faced accusations about misusing funds. These allegations, though false, showed the challenges of high-profile charitable work. The trust itself stepped forward to verify the legitimacy of their contributions.

Continued Commitment

While they stepped back from Christmas singles after 2022, their support for The Trussell Trust remained steady. Through continued brand partnerships, book sales, and public advocacy, they maintained their fight against food poverty. Their partnership had grown from a simple idea about sausage roll songs into a sustained campaign against hunger in Britain.

Lasting Change

The Hoyles transformed their platform into a force for positive change, proving entertainment and social responsibility could work hand in hand. Their partnership with The Trussell Trust showed how social media influence could translate into real-world impact. As food bank usage continued to rise, their work highlighted an ongoing crisis - one that required attention long after the Christmas songs stopped playing.

The relationship between LadBaby and The Trussell Trust demonstrated how creative thinking could address serious social issues. Through music, merchandise, and media appearances, they brought attention to food poverty while raising substantial funds. Their success proved that entertainment could serve a higher purpose, creating change while spreading joy.

Chapter 8: Beyond Social Media

Literary Beginnings

September 2021 marked a significant milestone when the Hoyles visited Greythorn Primary School - Mark's childhood school - to announce their first children's book. "Greg the Sausage Roll: Santa's Little Helper" would launch on November 11, 2021.

The choice of location carried special meaning, as both Mark and Roxanne had overcome dyslexia to become authors. Their announcement included a powerful admission about their learning differences, showing children that such challenges needn't limit achievement.

Educational Partnership

The Hoyles partnered with Puffin Books, WHSmith, and the National Literacy Trust for their literary debut. Their initiative ensured that for every book pre-ordered through WHSmith, another book reached a child who didn't own one. This commitment to literacy reflected their ongoing dedication to helping families while maintaining their charitable focus.

Greg's Growing Success

The sausage roll character captured young readers' imaginations. By November 2022, "Greg the Sausage Roll: The Perfect Present" reached number one on the Children's Bestseller List. The series expanded rapidly through 2023 and 2024, with "Wish You Were Here," "12 Days of Christmas," "Egg-cellent Easter

Adventure," and "Lunchbox Superhero" all maintaining charitable components through WHSmith sales.

Musical Education

Their board book "12 Days of Christmas" added new dimensions to children's education. "Research has shown that rhyme and singing play a vital role in children's development," the Hoyles explained, "fostering coordination, imagination, concentration, memory, confidence with language, and a love for reading." The book combined their Christmas music experience with educational goals.

Brand Extensions

October 2020 brought the launch of Walkers' sausage roll-flavored crisps. In 2021, Roxanne created an inclusive clothing range with In The Style, focusing on all sizes for mothers. The same year saw Euro 2020 themed clothing and the introduction of Greg the Sausage Roll soft toys. Each product maintained their commitment to accessibility and affordability.

Theme Park Magic

August 2024 saw an unusual honor - Alton Towers Resort renamed their Runaway Mine Train as 'The Wonderland Express' for two days to celebrate "Greg the Sausage Roll: The World's Funniest Unicorn." The event featured meet-and-greets with the Hoyles and book characters, bringing their creation to life for young fans.

Television Recognition

Their media presence spanned Britain's most-watched shows. Good Morning Britain, Lorraine, The One Show, and This Morning regularly featured the Hoyles. Their earliest television appearance came in 2012, when Roxanne participated in Channel 4's Hidden Talent, training with champion freediver Emma Farrell to hold her breath underwater for four minutes and eighteen seconds.

Award Winners

Recognition came early and often. June 2018 saw Mark win Clas Ohlson's "Celebrity Dad of the Year" award, beating Prince William in a public vote. Nine months later, Roxanne claimed "Celebrity Mum of the Year." October 2021 brought Mark a nomination for the Pride of

Britain Award in the ITV Charity Fundraiser of the Year category.

Publishing Impact

Their success carried additional weight given their personal challenges with dyslexia. Each new book maintained their charitable focus - their 2024 releases continued supporting The Trussell Trust through WHSmith sales. Their publishing success challenged industry skepticism about their credentials as authors.

Retail Innovation

Their merchandising strategy reflected their values - accessibility, affordability, and giving back. From books to clothing, each product served dual purposes: entertaining while supporting charitable causes. Their business decisions consistently aligned with their core principles of helping others while spreading joy.

Media Evolution

Their expansion demonstrated how social media influence could translate into traditional media success. They maintained authenticity across platforms, from television appearances to book signings. Their ability to adapt their message for different media while maintaining their core values set them apart from other influencers.

The Hoyles transformed from social media personalities into multi-platform entertainers and educators. Through books, merchandise, television appearances, and theme park attractions, they built a brand that maintained their original mission: helping families while creating joy.

Part IV: The Real Story

Chapter 9: The Dark Side of Fame

Learning the Hard Way

"There's no manual or education on how to deal with that," Roxanne reflected on their sudden rise to internet fame. The couple had to learn through trial and error how to handle public recognition. Mark admitted to The Guardian: "No one tells you what to do or how to do it, or how to handle getting recognised on the street. That was something we've had to learn on the job."

The initial days of content creation came with costly lessons about privacy. In their early videos, Mark would film their street and front door in Hemel Hempstead. "I think we never expected as many people to be watching," he later admitted. This innocent oversight would have serious consequences as their following grew to 13 million across social media platforms.

Unwanted Visitors

The reality of their exposure hit home when someone added their address to Google Maps. People began showing up at their house uninvited. "It was frightening," Mark recalled. When they reported these incidents, the police seemed unconcerned, suggesting only that they stop posting videos. The situation forced them to relocate to Nottingham, Mark's hometown.

The Blackmail Attempt

In early 2022, the Hoyles received messages via DM from an anonymous account demanding £5,000. The blackmailer threatened to release a video allegedly showing Mark inappropriately touching a woman in a Nottingham bar. When the Hoyles ignored the threat, the demand increased to £10,000. Months later, the video appeared on social media and got picked up by the press.

Fighting Back

The couple maintained the man in the grainy video wasn't Mark. Roxanne stated firmly: "I knew it wasn't Mark in the film. He knew it wasn't him." She pointed out the impossibility of the situation, noting they rarely went out without each other. The couple reported the blackmail attempt to the police, but the anonymous accounts vanished, leaving no trace.

Mental Health Impact

The constant scrutiny and attacks took their toll on Mark's mental health. He began experiencing panic attacks - a condition he continues to manage. "I think I always will, but I'm better at dealing with them now," he shared. "I can see them coming, I understand how they are."

Protecting Their Children

The Hoyles faced difficult decisions about their children's involvement in content creation. They established clear boundaries: their sons could choose whether to participate in videos. This explained why their older son appeared more frequently than their younger one, who disliked being photographed. The parents also had to teach their children about the reality of their public life: "My kids have experienced things they would never have experienced if me and Mark hadn't started LadBaby," Roxanne explained.

Physical Threats

The online harassment sometimes spilled into real-world confrontations. Mark faced a threatening situation in a pub that required bouncers to rush him into a taxi. The severity of threats escalated until anti-terror officers visited their home to provide security advice.

Online Abuse

Roxanne faced her own battles with trolls, particularly regarding her appearance. "I'd get a lot of abuse too from people saying, 'No wonder he's doing that, you're too fat,'" she revealed. The cruel comments about their children's appearances particularly affected the couple.

Police Involvement

Initially skeptical of their complaints, law enforcement eventually recognized the seriousness of the threats. The involvement of anti-terror officers marked a turning point in how authorities viewed their security concerns. The police presence during this period highlighted the real dangers they faced.

The price of fame had proven steeper than either Mark or Roxanne anticipated. Their story served as a cautionary tale about the dark side of social media success. Yet they refused to let these challenges drive them from their platform.

Instead, they adapted, learned, and continued their work - albeit with greater awareness of the risks involved in sharing their lives online.

Chapter 10: Staying True

The Wealth Question

Success brought financial security to the Hoyles, a dramatic shift from their days of £20 weekly food budgets. This change created an unexpected challenge: how to balance their newfound comfort with their advocacy for those in poverty. "We have felt really guilty about that," Mark admitted to The Guardian. "I feel terrible that I've moved into this lovely house at a time when people are really struggling."

Maintaining Perspective

Roxanne's approach to their improved circumstances remained grounded in their past experiences. She continued shopping at Poundland and Home Bargains, browsing for deals just as she had during their leaner years. "I still love a visit to Poundland," she told The Sun. "I don't wear designer clothes and you'll often catch me browsing the shelves of Home Bargains."

Transportation Choices

Their commitment to modest living extended to their vehicles. "Forget about fancy cars - we both drive standard runarounds," Roxanne shared. This decision reflected their broader philosophy about wealth: success didn't require flashy displays of affluence.

Class and Media

The Hoyles faced particular scrutiny as working-class creators in traditionally middle-class spaces. Mark observed that breaking into creative industries proved harder for working-class individuals. "I struggled at university," he noted. "I struggled in advertising." Their experience highlighted ongoing class barriers in British media.

Industry Pushback

The publishing and music industries often met their success with skepticism. "We get it," Roxanne acknowledged. "We're not credible music artists, but it was sad because a lot of people could have helped the charity." Even after their achievements, they encountered resistance at industry events. "There are still people that won't want you there, that don't believe you've worked for it."

Political Pressure

Initially, the Hoyles maintained political neutrality, focusing on entertainment and charity. "Our channels are just about doing silly videos and making people laugh," Mark explained. However, as food bank usage rose by 94% over five years, reaching 3.1 million parcels annually, they faced pressure to take stronger stances on government policies.

Speaking Out

In 2024, Mark finally addressed speculation about his political views. "I've always voted Labour," he revealed. "I come from a working-class background, I voted Labour at every election." This admission came after years of maintaining political privacy to focus on their charitable work.

Social Media Reality

The couple's approach to content remained consistent despite their success. They continued managing their own social media accounts rather than hiring teams. This hands-on approach meant they saw all comments - positive and negative - but maintained their direct connection with followers.

Family Values

Their definition of wealth shifted with success. Rather than measuring it in material terms, they valued time with family. Both parents could now attend school runs and witness their children's milestones - opportunities Mark had missed during his corporate career.

The Final Song

The decision to end their Christmas single streak came from a desire to preserve their original mission. "The last one became more about us than the charity," Mark explained. "It became more about us defending our decision to do it, and justifying where the money was going. It was taking away from the reason this started."

While they stepped back from Christmas songs, they maintained their commitment to accessibility and charitable giving. Each new venture - from books to brand collaborations - included elements of giving back. Roxanne noted the possibility of a return for their 10-year anniversary in 2028, hinting at a "sausage roll megamix."

Chapter 11: The Future of LadBaby

Literary Focus

2024 marked a year of literary expansion for the Hoyles. February saw the release of "Greg the Sausage Roll: Egg-cellent Easter Adventure," with WHSmith donating 50p to The Trussell Trust for each paperback sold.

Their World Book Day contribution, "Greg the Sausage Roll: Lunchbox Superhero," continued their commitment to children's literacy. Each book maintained their signature mix of entertainment and social responsibility.

Theme Park Adventures

August 2024 brought "Greg the Sausage Roll: The World's Funniest Unicorn" to life at Alton Towers Resort. The Runaway Mine Train's temporary transformation into 'The Wonderland Express' showed how their brand had grown from social media to real-world experiences. Meet-and-greets at the park allowed them to connect directly with young fans.

Family First

Nottingham life centers around their sons, Phoenix and Kobe. The move back to Mark's hometown provided stability after their security concerns in Hemel Hempstead. Their attic recording studio allows them to create content while staying close to family. Three times weekly, they broadcast live sessions to their paid subscribers, maintaining consistent connection with their audience.

Educational Impact

Their "12 Days of Christmas" board book showcases their new direction in children's education. "Research has shown that rhyme and singing play a vital role in children's development," the Hoyles explained, "fostering coordination, imagination, concentration, memory, confidence with language, and a love for reading." Their experience with Christmas number ones now serves educational purposes.

Christmas Future

While they've stepped away from Christmas singles, Roxanne hasn't ruled out a return. The 10-year anniversary of their first hit approaches in 2028, and she's mentioned the possibility of a "sausage roll megamix." Mark remains more cautious, though he joked about helping Mariah Carey achieve another Christmas number one.

Social Media Evolution

Their online presence continues growing, with 13 million followers across platforms. Live streaming creates real-time connections with fans, while their podcast reaches audiences in a more intimate format. They maintain their own social media management, preserving the direct relationship with followers that built their success.

Charitable Commitment

The Trussell Trust partnership endures through their publishing ventures. Their February 2024 book release included charitable donations up to £10,000. This approach shows their determination to fight food poverty, even without Christmas singles.

Brand Development

Their business model focuses on accessibility and affordability. Roxanne's clothing collaborations maintain inclusive sizing, while their books and merchandise stay reasonably priced. Each venture includes charitable elements, showing how commerce and conscience can work together.

Message of Hope

"We're positive people, we're joyful," Roxanne told the media in 2024. Their story, she emphasized, shows how determination can overcome obstacles. "There's chapters that are really positive, and then we talk about some of the things that have happened and the fake stories. For us, it was a bit like therapy – this is a positive book about two people that have overcome and done things they should never have done."

Mark reflects on their unlikely success with wonder. "I never thought I'd have one song in the charts – I'm not someone who can sing, so the fact I've had a song that went to number one for charity once, never mind five times, is pretty mind-blowing." This attitude of grateful surprise remains central to their approach.

The Hoyles continue expanding their influence while remaining true to their original mission: helping families while spreading joy. As they build their legacy through books, brand partnerships, and charitable work, they maintain the down-to-earth approach that first endeared them to millions.

Epilogue: The LadBaby Effect

Reshaping Social Media

The LadBaby phenomenon transformed how social media personalities approach content creation. Using the same free editing app from their first viral video through years of success, they showed that expensive equipment wasn't necessary for meaningful content. Their three weekly live sessions demonstrated how direct audience engagement could build lasting connections.

The Numbers That Matter

The Trussell Trust partnership set new standards for social media fundraising. Their Christmas singles generated £305,000, while brand partnerships pushed their total contribution past £1.3 million. These figures created a blueprint for turning social media influence into concrete charitable impact. Their collaboration with Walkers crisps, where five pence from each packet went to charity, showed how brand deals could serve social good.

Christmas Revolution

Five consecutive Christmas number ones rewrote British music history. Breaking The Beatles' previous record of four, they proved novelty songs could compete with mainstream artists. Their collaborations brought established stars like Ed Sheeran and Elton John into charitable projects. As Sheeran told them during their collaboration: "I hope you two never change." Their success created new traditions, with families worldwide gathering to hear their Christmas countdown.

Class Barriers Broken

The Hoyles challenged class-based assumptions in British media. As working-class creators entering middle-class dominated spaces, they faced industry skepticism. Yet their achievements - from chart records to bestselling books - proved talent transcends social barriers. Their experience struggling at university and in advertising resonated with others facing similar obstacles. "It's harder for working-class people to break into a lot of industries," Mark noted, highlighting ongoing challenges while proving they could be overcome.

Educational Innovation

Their "Greg the Sausage Roll" series revolutionized children's publishing. Each book maintained their commitment to accessibility, with charitable components built into sales. Their board book "12 Days of Christmas" merged entertainment with education, using their music experience to boost child development. The WHSmith partnership ensured books reached children who couldn't afford them, creating a model for inclusive literacy programs.

Family First Philosophy

The Hoyles redefined social media success by prioritizing family values. Their approach to children's privacy - letting their sons choose their level of involvement - set standards for family content creators. They proved content creation could coexist with responsible parenting, maintaining boundaries while sharing authentic moments.

Financial Transparency

Their openness about money matters - from early struggles with £20 weekly food budgets to managing later success - provided a manual for responsible influence. They showed how to handle wealth while advocating for those in need, maintaining credibility through consistent charitable work and modest living. Their continued shopping at discount stores demonstrated authenticity in action.

Cultural Impact

The Hoyles' influence extended beyond social media into British popular culture. Their sausage roll theme carried through music, books, and even theme park attractions. The Alton Towers collaboration in 2024 showed how digital influence could translate into real-world experiences. Their story became part of modern British cultural history, proving entertainment and social responsibility could work hand in hand.

Setting Standards

Their handling of fame's darker aspects - from privacy violations to blackmail attempts - created a roadmap for other creators facing similar challenges. They showed how to maintain authenticity under pressure, handle criticism constructively, and prioritize mental health while building a brand.

Lasting Message

The LadBaby story proves that ordinary people can create extraordinary change. From a £4 toolbox video to record-breaking charity campaigns, they showed how creativity and compassion could reshape popular culture. Their legacy lives in the millions raised for food banks, the barriers broken for working-class creators, and the example set for responsible social media influence. As Mark observed: "Everyone should be in a position where they can afford the essentials in life. If that's not Christmas spirit, then I don't know what is."

The End.

Printed in Great Britain
by Amazon